Wild Goose Chase Quilts

Eleanor Burns

For Father, Erwin Knoechel, who taught me to Fly!

First printing April, 2001

Published by Quilt in a Day®, Inc.
1955 Diamond St, San Marcos, CA 92069

©2001 by Eleanor A. Burns Family Trust

ISBN 1-891776-06-1

Art Director Merritt Voigtlander

Contents

Light Geese with Two Fabrics

Light Geese with Scrappy Fabrics

Light Geese with Multi Fabrics

Dark Geese with Three Fabrics

Dark Geese with Fussy Cut

Geese in Positive and Negative

Introduction

I have fond memories of standing in my yard with Father in Zelienople, Pennsylvania, when a flock of geese that had gathered in the adjacent pasture took flight. What a magnificent sight! They weren't more than twenty feet over our heads - gathering into their V formation, flapping their wings, honking loudly from behind. It was at that moment I clearly saw the Flying Geese quilt patch!

When my husband "dragged" me from our Pennsylvania home to California in 1975, I felt like the thousands of pioneer women before me, who reluctantly climbed into the wagon seat, and tearfully said "Goodbye" to their loving family. We all were on a "wild goose chase" to a fresh start - a migration to North, South, East, and West!

The Wild Goose Chase block is so versatile, we flew in a number of different directions with color variations and arrangement of patches. There are five different versions to chose from, and, you may even come up with your own personal flight!

Wherever you migrate, may you flock together with your quilting friends!

Honk if you love Quilting!

Antique Quilt

4

Selecting Your Design

Light Geese with Two Fabrics *Fabric selection and yardage for these quilts begin on page 12.*

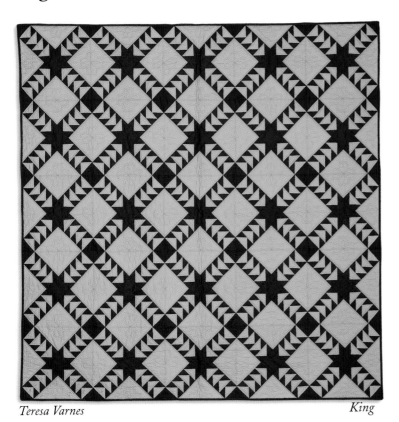

Teresa Varnes   *King*

Patricia Knoechel   *12 blocks*

The Wild Goose Chase quilt is typical of quilts made in Turkey Red and white in the 1800s. Turkey Red was popular with quilters because it was a fast color, and did not run or bleed when it was washed.

Teresa Varnes recreated this beautiful "timeless" quilt from a photograph of an antique quilt. Light Geese fly into the Turkey Red center, creating a spectacular star shape. Red Corner Triangles join together to form a magnificent secondary pattern.

The geometric lines of the Wild Goose Chase are particularly appropriate for traditional blue and white fabrics as well.

Patricia Knoechel's outstanding quilt has a fresh, clean look. Its cool contemporary design could compliment modern decor as well as refresh a country home.

For authenticity, Teresa and Patty choose not to add Borders. The intricate machine quilting by Carol Selepec adds to the appeal of these classic quilts.

Light Geese with Scrappy Fabrics
Yardage and instructions begin on page 30.

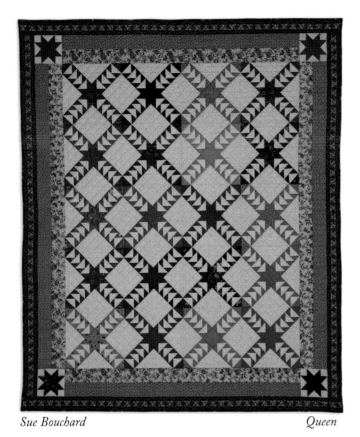

Sue Bouchard   *Queen*

Light Geese with Multiple Fabrics
Yardage and instructions begin on page 38.

Patricia Knoechel   *Twin*

Sue Bouchard's beautiful quilt, made in 1855-1870 Civil War reproduction fabrics designed by Nancy Kirk for Benartex, duplicates the charm of antique quilts! She selected one nostalgic beige Background fabric in an overall scroll design for the Geese and Side Triangles. Sewing one block at a time, Sue selected twenty different prints for the remaining patchwork. A traditional Star Border with final Stripe exemplifies the beauty of this "old time" quilt!

Patricia Knoechel selected multiple fabrics for her rich, contemporary Wild Goose Chase Quilt. For a stunning adaptation, she made two different Star blocks, one in five different values of blue, and one in five different values of purple. All Geese are celestial white, surrounded by light textured Side Triangles which pull the blues and purples together. By selecting the Sky in different values, the Geese appear to be flying into the Star from a distance. Simple Borders enhance the beauty of the blocks. Sandy Thompson long arm machine quilted a simple but elegant design in the Side Triangles.

Dark Geese with Fussy Cuts
Fussy cut instructions are on page 11.

Patricia Knoechel   *Wallhanging*

Dark Geese with Three Fabrics
Yardage and instructions for both quilts begin on page 46.

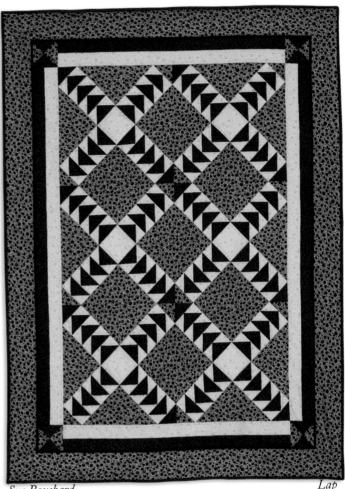

Sue Bouchard   *Lap*

Patricia Knoechel selected bright spring time colors and a handful of fussy cut flowers for the center of each block. Accented by the cloud white Sky, Blue Geese fly away from the dark floral center. Side Triangles the color of sunshine pull pieces all together. Fussy cut flowers are repeated in the Borders.

Teresa Varnes stippled the large florals in the Side Triangles.

Sue Bouchard selected a patriotic theme with navy blue Geese flying in all directions from a beige center. Americana red, beige, and blue Side Triangles surround the Geese in flight. Patchwork designs created when blocks join are repeated in the Borders. Straight lines simplify the grid quilting!

Light and Dark Geese in Positive/Negative Fabrics

Yardage and instructions begin on page 66.

Eleanor Burns

Twin

Eleanor Burns created this striking quilt from a photograph of an antique quilt made in Pennsylvania in 1890.

Only two fabrics are used, but the positive-negative effect of the two blocks offers a dynamic graphic look. Dark Geese and dark Side Triangles make up half of the blocks, with light Geese and light Side Triangles making up the second set.

Eleanor's cousin, Carol Selepec, long arm quilted this handsome variation with graceful feathers!

Supplies

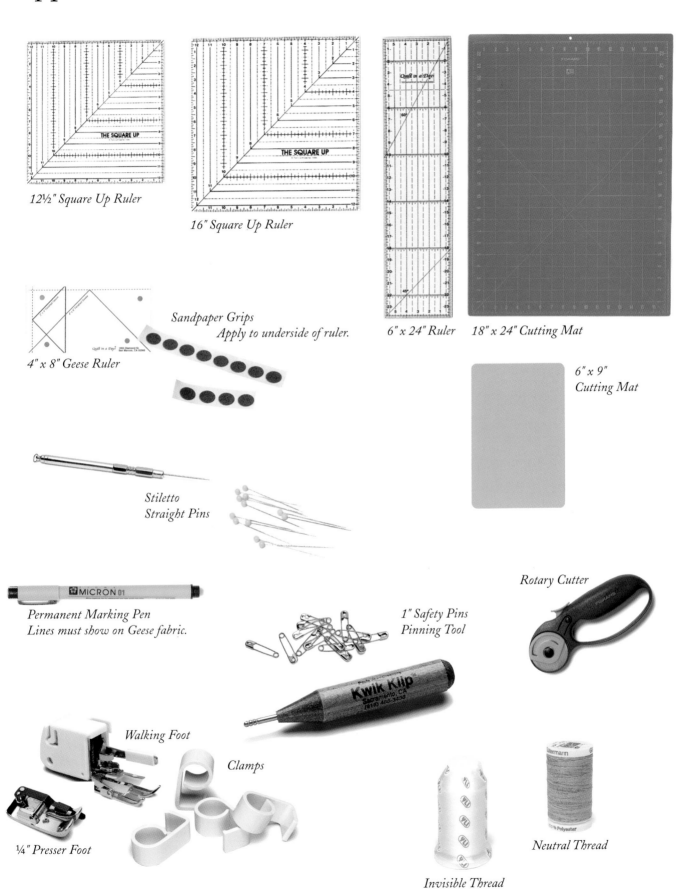

12½" Square Up Ruler

16" Square Up Ruler

6" x 24" Ruler

18" x 24" Cutting Mat

4" x 8" Geese Ruler

Sandpaper Grips
Apply to underside of ruler.

6" x 9"
Cutting Mat

Stiletto
Straight Pins

Permanent Marking Pen
Lines must show on Geese fabric.

1" Safety Pins
Pinning Tool

Rotary Cutter

Walking Foot

Clamps

¼" Presser Foot

Invisible Thread

Neutral Thread

Cutting Squares

1. Cut a nick in one selvage, the tightly woven edge on both sides of the fabric. Tear across the grain from selvage to selvage.

2. Press fabric, particularly the torn edge.

3. Fold fabric in half, matching the frayed edges. Don't worry about the selvages lining up correctly as this is not always possible.

4. Lay fabric on cutting mat with most of it to the right. Make sure torn edge is lined up at the left. Lay the ¼" line on 6" x 24" ruler along the torn edge, and trim.

5. Reposition ruler, line up designated strip width, and cut.

6. Turn strip and square off selvage edges. Layer cut two squares in designated size.

7. Repeat until you have the desired number of squares.

Leftover pieces on strips can be cut into smaller squares on yardage charts.

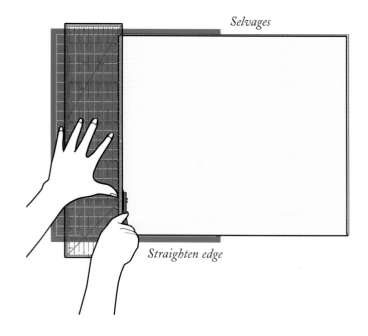

Selvages

Straighten edge

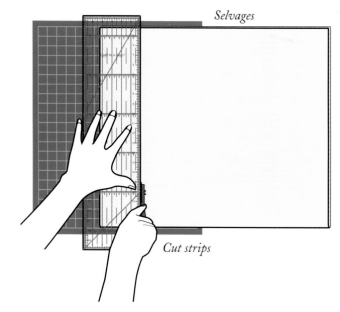

Selvages

Cut strips

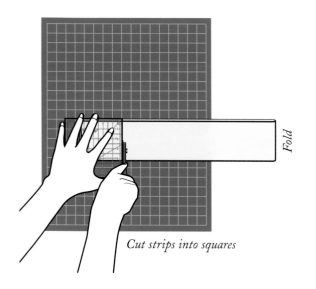

Fold

Cut strips into squares

Fussy Cuts

Add interest to your quilt with fussy cuts, large scale flowers centered on the patches. Center Squares are fussy cuts on point and Border Corners are straight fussy cuts.

1. Select a large scale print approximately 3½" square that coordinates with Geese and Side Triangles.

2. Cut two 4½" squares from template plastic. Cut 8½" squares for Border Corners on Twin, Queen and King Quilts.

3. Center on selected print for fussy cut, placing template for Center Square on point, and template for Border Corners on straight.

4. Trace fussy cuts on templates with permanent marking pen.

5. Move template, line up fussy cut, mark around template, and cut out. Make one Center Square per Wild Goose block, and four Border Corners.

Fussy Cut   *Teresa Varnes*

4½" Center Squares for Blocks

4½" Border Corners for Wallhangings and Lap

8½" Border Corners for Twin, Queen and King

Light Geese with Two Fabrics

Select these fabrics.

One Light Fabric for Geese

The same fabric is also used in Side Triangles and First Border. The example shown is solid country beige.

One Dark Fabric for Sky

The same fabric is also used in Center Square, Corner Triangles, Second Border, and Binding.

For an antique look, select a small scale floral or design that reads solid from a distance.

The example shown is a small red dotted fabric designed by Nancy Kirk for Benartex.

Four light Geese point toward the dark Center Square, forming a Star. When blocks are set together, a secondary pattern appears as a square on point.

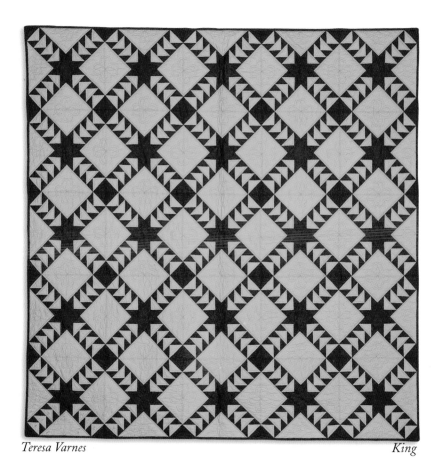

Teresa Varnes *King*

Sky
Center Square
Corner Triangles

Geese
Side Triangles

Finished Block *17" x 17"*

12

Paste-Up Sheet – Two Fabrics

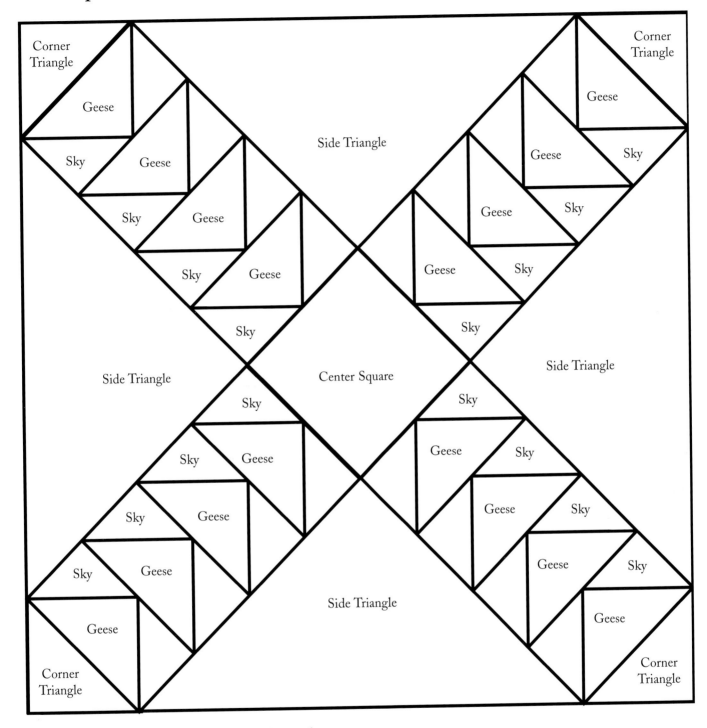

These measurements are for your Paste-Up Sheet only.

Cut swatches from your fabric and paste in place with a glue stick.

Light

Geese
(8) 1⅛" ◹

Side Triangles
(2) 3¼" ◹

Dark

Sky
(16) ¾" ◹

Center Square
(1) 1⅝" ▫

Corner Triangles
(1) 1⅛" ◹

Two Fabric Quilt

Cut strips selvage to selvage.
Cut squares from strips. Left over strips can be cut
into smaller size squares on yardage chart.

		One Block	**Four Block**	**Lap**
Geese		½ yd	1 ½ yds	2 yds
	Side Triangles	(1) 13" sq	(2) 13" strips cut into (4) 13" sqs	(2) 13" strips cut into (6) 13" sqs
	Geese	(4) 5½" sqs	(3) 5½" strips into (16) 5½" sqs	(4) 5 1/2" strips into (24) 5½" sqs
	First Border	(2) 1½" strips	(4) 2½" strips	(5) 2 ½" strips
Sky		½ yd	1 ½ yds	1 ¾ yds
	Sky	(4) 7" sqs	(4) 7" strips cut into (16) 7" sqs	(4) 7" strips cut into (24) 7" sqs
	Center Square	(1) 4½" sq	(1) 4½" strip cut into (4) 4½" sqs	(1) 4 ½" strip cut into (6) 4 ½" sqs
	Corner Triangles	(2) 4" sqs	(1) 4" strip cut into (8) 4" sqs	(2) 4" strips cut into (12) 4" sqs
	Second Border	(3) 3" strips	(4) 3 ½" strips	(5) 3 ½" strips
Finishing				
Binding		⅓ yd	½ yd	⅝ yd
		(3) 3" strips	(5) 3" strips	(6) 3" strips
Backing		1 yd	2 ½ yds	3 yds
Batting		30" x 30"	50" x 50"	52" x 69"

1 Block	1 Block	24" x 24"
4 Block	4 Blocks	42" x 42"
Lap	6 Blocks	42" x 59"
Twin	15 Blocks	66" x 100"
Queen	20 Blocks	91" x 108"
King	25 Blocks	108" x 108"

Twin	Queen	King

4 ¼ yds
(5) 13" strips cut into
    (15) 13" sqs
(9) 5½" strips cut into
    (60) 5½" sqs
(8) 3½" strips
	6 yds
	(7) 13" strips cut into
	    (20) 13" sqs
	(12) 5½" strips cut into
	    (80) 5½" sqs
	(9) 5½" strips
		7 ¼ yds
		(9) 13" strips cut into
		    (25) 13" sqs
		(15) 5½" strips cut into
		    (100) 5½" sqs
		(10) 5½" strips

4 yds
(10) 7" strips cut into
    (60) 7" sqs
(2) 4½" strips cut into
    (15) 4½" sqs
(3) 4" strips cut into
    (30) 4" sqs
(8) 5½" strips
	6 yds
	(14) 7" strips cut into
	    (80) 7" sqs
	(3) 4½" strips cut into
	    (20) 4½" sqs
	(4) 4" strips cut into
	    (40) 4" sqs
	(10) 7½" strips
		6 ¾ yds
		(17) 7" strips cut into
		    (100) 7" sqs
		(3) 4½" strip cut into
		    (25) 4½" sqs
		(5) 4" strips cut into
		    (50) 4" sqs
		(10) 7½" strips

⅞ yd (9) 3" strips	**1 yd** (10) 3" strips	**1 yd** (11) 3" strips
6¼ yds	**8 ½ yds**	**9 ¾ yds**
75" x 109"	100" x 117"	117" x 117"

Making 2" x 4" Light Geese

1. Place 5½" light Geese square right sides together and centered on 7" dark Sky square. Press.

Each set makes four Geese.

2. Place 6" x 12" ruler on squares so ruler touches all four corners. Draw diagonal line across squares.

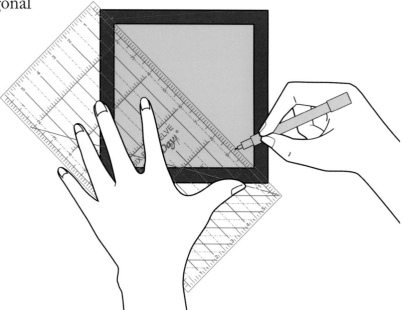

3. Pin.

4. Sew **exactly** ¼" from drawn line. Use 15 stitches per inch or 2.0 on computerized machines. Assembly-line sew several squares.

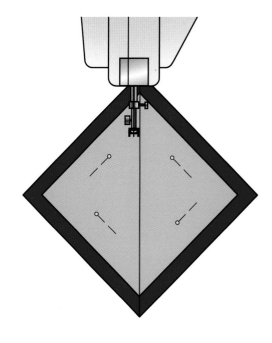

5. Turn and sew ¼" seam from second side of drawn line. Press to set seam.

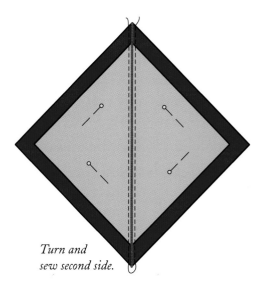

Turn and sew second side.

6. Remove pins. Cut on drawn line.

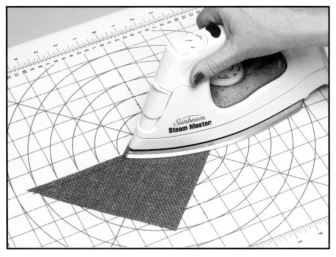

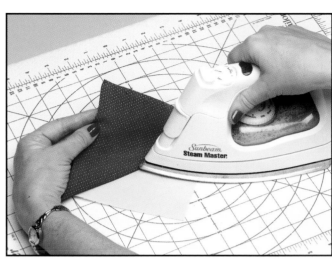

7. Place on pressing mat with **large triangle** on top. Press to set seam.

8. Open and press flat. Check that there are no tucks, and **seam is pressed toward larger triangle.**

Seams are pressed toward larger triangle.

9. Place pieces right sides together so that opposite fabrics touch with Geese matched to Sky. **Seams are parallel with each other.**

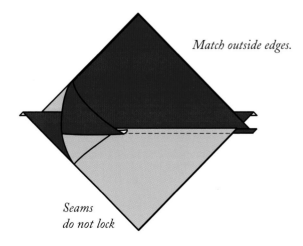

Match outside edges.

10. Match up outside edges. Notice that there is a gap between seams. **The seams do not lock.**

Seams do not lock

11. Draw a diagonal line across seams. Pin.

12. Sew ¼" from both sides of drawn line. Hold seams flat with stiletto so seams do not flip. Press to set seam.

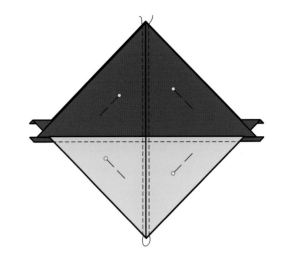

13. Cut on the drawn line.

14. Clip the seam allowance to the vertical seam midway between the horizontal seams. This allows the seam allowance to be pressed away from Geese.

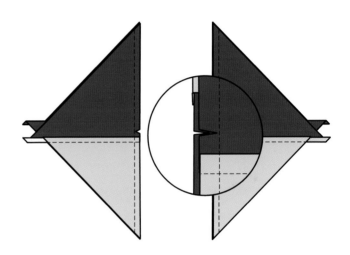

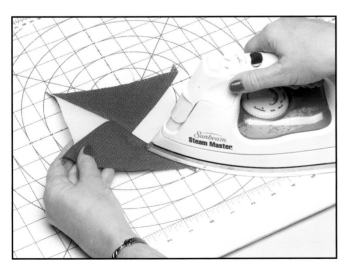

15. From right side, press into one Geese. Turn and press into second Geese seam.

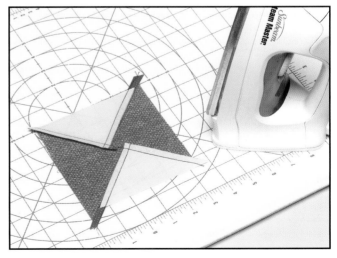

16. Turn over, and press on wrong side. At clipped seam, fabric is pressed away from Geese.

Squaring Up With Geese Ruler

1. Place Geese on small cutting mat so you can rotate mat as you cut.

2. Use the Large Flying Geese ruler. Line up ruler's 2" x 4" **red lines** on 45° sewn lines. Line up dotted line with peak of triangle for the ¼" seam allowance.

3. Cut block in half to separate the two patches.

Cut block in half.

4. Trim off excess fabric on right. Hold ruler securely on fabric so it will not shift while cutting.

5. Turn patch around. **Do not turn ruler.** Trim off excess fabric on right.

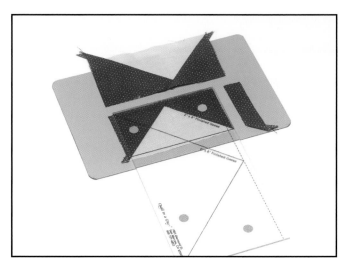

Trim off excess fabric on right.

Total Number of Geese Needed	
1 Block Wallhanging	16
4 Block Wallhanging	64
Lap	96
Twin	240
Queen	320
King	400

Turn patch. Trim off excess on right.

Squaring Up Without Geese Ruler

1. With a 6" x 12" ruler, line up the 45° line on a Geese seam, and the ¼" line on the peak.

2. Cut across, keeping an exact ¼" seam allowance beyond peak.

3. Turn second piece and repeat. A small strip will be cut out of center. Stack. Set the 6" x 12" ruler aside.

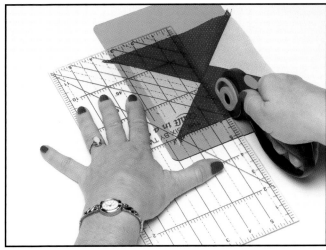

Cut block in half.

4. With the 6" square ruler, place the diagonal line on the seam. Line up the bottom edge of the Geese with the 2½" line on the ruler. Left edge should be slightly wider than 4½". Trim right and top edges.

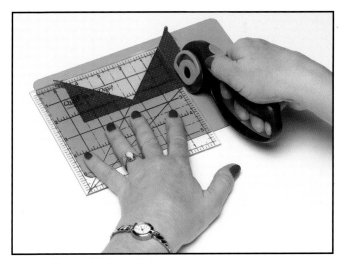

Trim off excess fabric on right.

5. Turn Geese patch. **Do not turn ruler**. Line up left edge on **2½" x 4½"** lines. Trim on right edge.

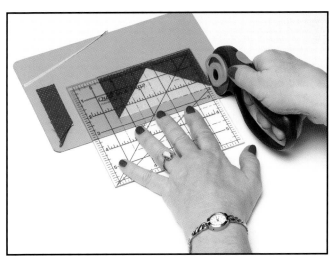

Turn patch. Trim off excess on right.

Sewing Light Geese Together

1. Divide Geese into two equal stacks.

2. Flip Goose patch on right to Goose patch on left. Match outside edges.

3. Hold seam flat with stiletto. Sew accurate ¼" seam, crossing point as you stitch.

4. Check to see that point is "crisp" on right side.

5. Assembly-line sew all Geese into pairs. Clip connecting threads.

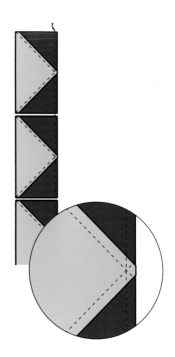

6. Divide into two equal stacks.

7. Sew together into sets of four. Clip connecting threads.

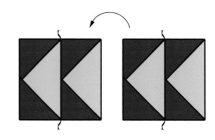

Sets of Four	
1 Block Wallhanging	4
4 Block Wallhanging	16
Lap	24
Twin	60
Queen	80
King	100

Pressing Geese

1. Place on pressing mat wrong side
   up. Press seams from base toward
   point of Geese.

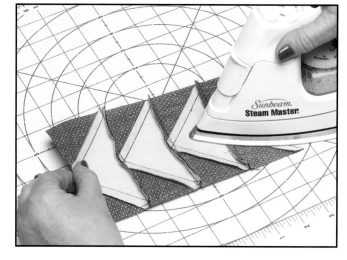

2. Press on right side, making certain there
   are no tucks at seams.

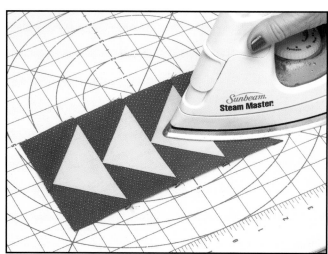

Adding Corner Triangles to Light Geese

1. Cut 4" dark squares for Corner Triangles
   in half on one diagonal, and **stack right
   side up.** You need one triangle for each
   set of four Geese.

2. **Stack Geese wrong side up and Corner
   Triangles right sides up.**

3. **Slide** Corners under Geese, and center.

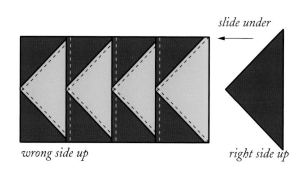

slide under

wrong side up

right side up

4. Assembly-line sew with ¼" seam, keeping tips equal on outside edges. Clip connecting threads.

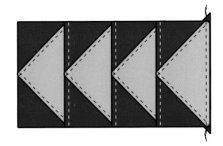

5. Place on pressing mat with Triangles on top. Set seams, open, and press. Seams are pressed toward Triangle.

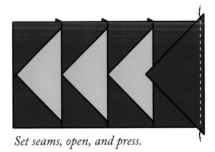

Set seams, open, and press.

6. Line up Geese ruler with outside edges of Geese, and trim off tips.
   Alternate: Use 6" Square Up ruler.

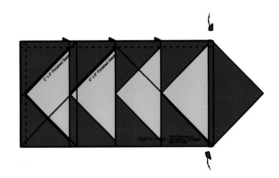

Sewing Center Squares to Light Geese

1. Stack 4½" Center Squares right side up. Stack an equal number of Geese wrong side up. You need one per block.

2. **Slide Center Squares under Geese.**

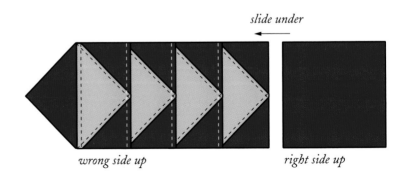

slide under

wrong side up   *right side up*

3. Match outside edges, and assembly-line sew. Cross point as you stitch. Check to see that point is "crisp" on right side.

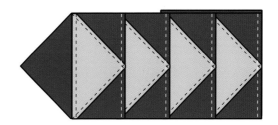

4. Set seams with Center Square on top. Open, and press seam flat. Clip connecting threads.

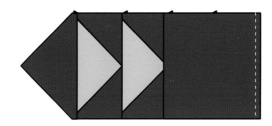

5. Sew Geese with Corner Triangles on opposite side of Square.

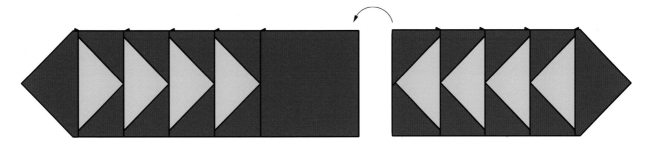

6. Set seams with Center Square on top. Open, and press seams flat. Seams will be toward Center Square.

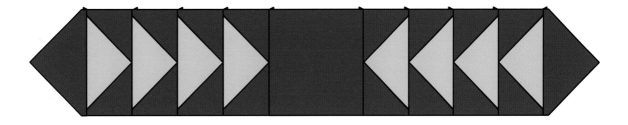

Sewing Block Together

1. Stretch edges of each 13" Side Triangle square. Stack with stretch at top and bottom, right side up. With 6" x 24" ruler, cut on both diagonals into quarters.

2. Separate into four equal stacks. **Mark all top and bottom triangles with safety pins. Keep safety pins in triangles until after top is sewn together.**

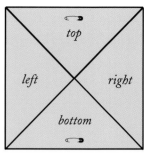

Its important to keep triangles in order because they stretch in opposite directions.

3. Place an equal number of Geese in center of stacks. Work on one half at a time.

4. Flip Geese to Side Triangle on left. Match top edges and sides. Side Triangle fabric will stick out on bottom edge.

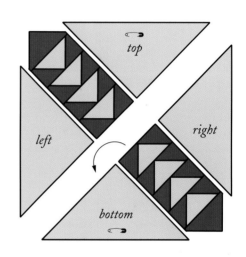

5. Assembly-line sew, using stiletto to hold seams flat.

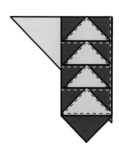

Edges of Side Triangles are on the bias, and should always be sewn on the bottom to avoid stretching.

6. Flip remaining Side Triangle to Geese. Match top edges and sides. Pin in place.

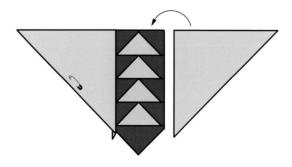

7. **Turn over to wrong side.** Sew from Corner Triangle, using stiletto to hold seams flat.

8. Place on pressing mat with Side Triangles on top. Press to set seams.

9. Open, and press flat. Seams will be toward Side Triangles.

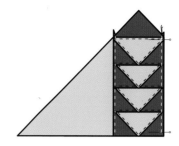
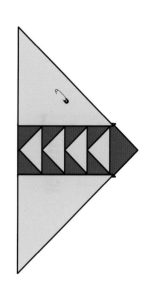

10. Lay out three units. Place Side Triangles with Center strip.

11. Flip Center to left. Match and pin center seams. Pin Geese to Side Triangles. Assembly-line sew with Side Triangles on bottom, holding seams flat with stiletto.

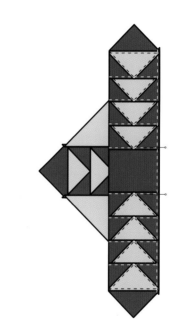

12. Flip Center strip to remaining Side Triangles. Pin, and assembly-line sew with Side Triangles on bottom.

13. Place on pressing mat right side up. Press to set seams. Open, and press seams flat. Center seams will be toward Side Triangles.

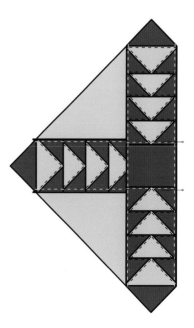

Squaring Up Blocks

1. Using grid lines, place block straight on cutting mat. Place 6" x 24" ruler on side of block. Line up ruler's ¼" lines on seams. Line up diagonal line down center of Geese. Straighten side.

2. Turn and trim remaining sides. Note measurement of block with lines on grid. Block should be approximately 17" square.

3. Trim all blocks consistently.

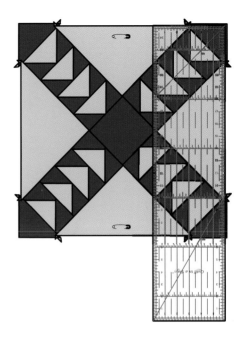

Sewing top Together

1. Lay out blocks. Place Side Triangles with safety pins at top and bottom so stretch on Side Triangles is the same.

2. Flip block on right to block on left.

3. Match and pin seams. Sew with ¼" seam.

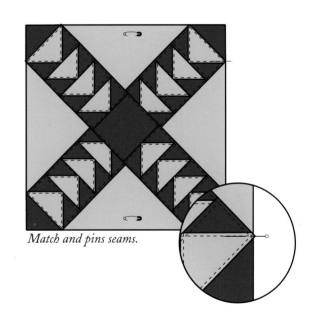

Match and pins seams.

Block Layout	
4 Block Wallhanging	2 x 2
Lap	2 x 3
Twin	3 x 5
Queen	4 x 5
King	5 x 5

4. Pin and sew all blocks in row together. Press seams in one direction.

5. Lay out rows with seams going in opposite directions.

6. Pin and sew rows together.

7. Press.

Turn to page 72 for finishing.

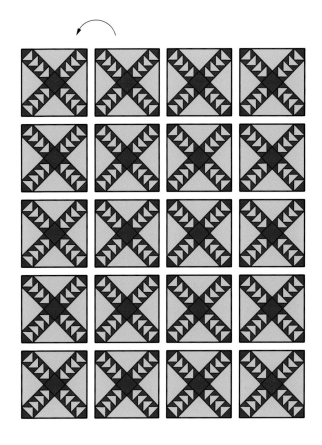

Light Geese
with Scrappy Fabrics

Select these fabrics.

One Light Fabric for Geese

The same fabric is also used as Side Triangles and Background for Border Stars. The sample is a reproduction 1855-1870 Civil War fabric in a scroll design that reads solid from a distance with flecks of multiple colors.

Different Darks and Mediums

Quarter yard pieces are enough for Sky, Center Square, and Corner Triangles. Fat quarters also work. Select one for each block, plus one additional third yard for Border Stars. Fabrics are easier to coordinate if they are pulled from the same line. Vary scales of prints, as large scale, small scale, and ones that read solid from a distance.

When light Geese are sewn pointing toward the dark Center Square, a Star is formed in the center of each block.

Two Border Fabrics

These fabrics may be repeats of two Sky fabrics, or may be entirely different fabrics. Widths of both Borders are 4½", and when sewn together, the strips must equal 8½", the size of the Border Stars.

Optional Striped Border Fabric

Strip may be any width to increase your quilt to desired size. Purchase fabric the length of the quilt.

Sue Bouchard   *Queen*

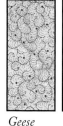

Geese *Sky* *Stars* *First Border* *Second Border* *Striped Border*

Finished Block   *17" x 17"*

Paste-Up Sheet – Scrappy Fabrics

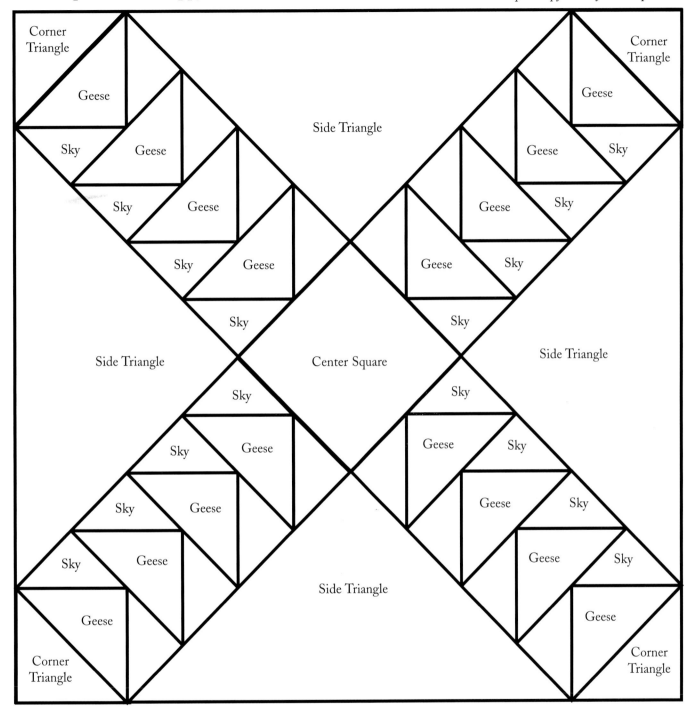

These measurements are for your Paste-Up Sheet only.

Cut swatches from your fabrics and paste in place with a glue stick.

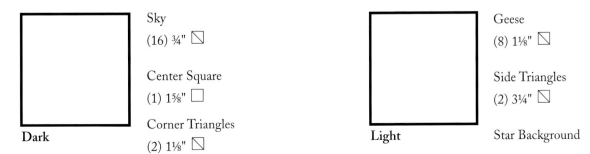

Sky
(16) ¾" ◨

Center Square
(1) 1⅝" ▢

Corner Triangles
(2) 1⅛" ◨

Dark

Geese
(8) 1⅛" ◨

Side Triangles
(2) 3¼" ◨

Star Background

Light

Scrappy Fabric Quilt

Cut strips selvage to selvage.
Cut squares from strips. Left over strips can be cut
into smaller size squares on yardage chart.
Fat quarters work well.

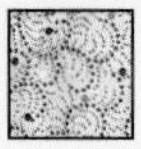

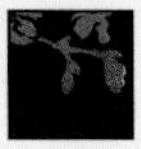

		Four Block	Lap
Light Geese		1 ½ yds	1 ¾ yds
	Side Triangles	(2) 13" strips cut into	(2) 13" strips cut into
		(4) 13" sqs	(6) 13" sqs
	Geese	(3) 5½" strips cut into	(4) 5½" strips cut into
		(16) 5½" sqs	(24) 5½" sqs
	Border Stars	(4) 5½" sqs	(4) 5½" sqs
		(1) 2½" strip cut into	(1) 2½" strip cut into
		(16) 2½" sqs	(16) 2½" sqs
Dark Scrappy Sky		**(4) different ¼ yd pieces**	**(6) different ¼ yd pieces**
		Cut from each piece	Cut from each piece
	Sky	(4) 7" sqs	(4) 7" sqs
	Center Square	(1) 4½" sq	(1) 4½" sq
	Corner Triangles	(2) 4" sqs	(2) 4" sqs
Dark Border Stars		⅓ yd	⅓ yd
	Star Points	(4) 7" sqs	(4) 7" sqs
	Center Square	(4) 4½" sqs	(4) 4½" sqs
Finishing			
	First Border	¾ yd	¾ yd
		(4) 4½" strips	(5) 4½" strips
	Second Border	¾ yd	¾ yd
		(4) 4½" strips	(5) 4½" strips
	Third Border or Stripe		
Binding		½ yd	⅝ yd
		(5) 3" strips	(6) 3" strips
Backing		3 ¼ yds	3 ¼ yds
Batting		56" x 56"	56" x 72"

4 Block	4 Blocks	50" x 50"
Lap	6 Blocks	50" x 66"
Twin	15 Blocks	73" x 106"
Queen	20 Blocks	89" x 106"
King	25 Blocks	106" x 106"

Twin	Queen	King

3 ¾ yds
(5) 13" strips cut into
    (15) 13" sqs
(9) 5½" strips cut into
    (60) 5½" sqs
(4) 5½" sqs
(1) 2½" strip cut into
    (16) 2½" sqs
	4 ¾ yds
	(7) 13" strips cut into
	    (20) 13" sqs
	(12) 5½" strips cut into
	    (80) 5½" sqs
	(4) 5½" sqs
	(1) 2½" strip cut into
	    (16) 2½" sqs
		6 yds
		(9) 13" strips cut into
		    (25) 13" sqs
		(15) 5½" strips cut into
		    (100) 5½" sqs
		(4) 5½" sqs
		(1) 2½" strip cut into
		    (16) 2½" sqs

(15) different ¼ yd pieces Cut from each piece (4) 7" sqs (1) 4½" sq (2) 4" sqs	**(20) different ¼ yd pieces** Cut from each piece (4) 7" sqs (1) 4½" sq (2) 4" sqs	**(25) different ¼ yd pieces** Cut from each piece (4) 7" sqs (1) 4½" sq (2) 4" sqs
⅓ yd (4) 7" sqs (4) 4½" sqs	⅓ yd (4) 7" sqs (4) 4½" sqs	⅓ yd (4) 7" sqs (4) 4½" sqs
1 yd (7) 4½" strips	1 ¼ yds (8) 4½" strips	1 ¼ yds (9) 4½" strips
1 yd (7) 4½" strips	1 ¼ yds (8) 4½" strips	1 ¼ yds (9) 4½" strips
1 ¼ yds (9) 4½" strips or 3 yds 4 strips cut lengthwise	1 ½ yds (10) 4½" strips or 3 ¼ yds 4 strips cut lengthwise	1 ½ yds (11) 4½" strips or 3 ¼ yds 4 strips cut lengthwise
⅞ yd (9) 3" strips	1 yd (10) 3" strips	1 yd (11) 3" strips
7 yds	8 ½ yds	10 yds
81" x 115"	98" x 115"	115" x 115"

Scrappy Quilts with Light Geese

1. Sort fabrics to sew on one block at a time. You need these pieces for one block:

Light Fabric	Same Medium or Dark Fabric
(4) 5½" Geese squares	(4) 7" Sky squares
(1) 13" Side Triangles Square	(1) 4½" Center Square
	(2) 4" Corner Triangles

Sew ¼" on left side.
Turn and sew second side.

2. Place 5½" Geese squares right sides together to 7" Sky squares. You should have four sets per block.

3. Sew 2" x 4" Light Geese, following detailed sewing directions beginning on page 16. Make four sets of four.

4. Add 4" Corner Triangles to Light Geese.

5. Sew 4½" Center Square to Geese.

6. Sew pieces together with Side Triangles.

7. Square up block.

Making Four Border Stars

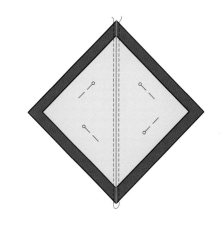

1. Place 5½" light Star squares right sides together to 7" dark Star Points. You should have four sets.

2. Make (16) 2" x 4" Light Geese. Follow sewing directions beginning on page 16.

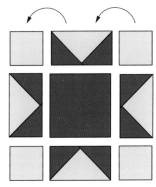

3. Make stacks of four with 4½" Center Squares and 2½" light corner squares.

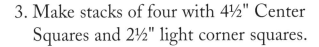

4. Flip top pieces in middle row onto top pieces on left row.

5. Assembly-line sew pieces right sides together.

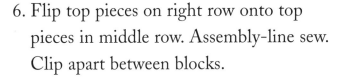

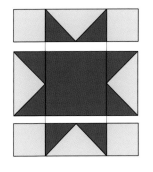
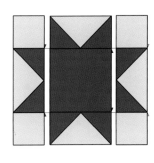

6. Flip top pieces on right row onto top pieces in middle row. Assembly-line sew. Clip apart between blocks.

7. Press seams away from Geese patches.

8. Sew rows right sides together, locking seams.

9. Press seams toward center.

Sewing Top Together

1. Lay out blocks, placing blocks so similar fabrics or values are not next to each other.

Block Layout	
4 Block Wallhanging	2 x 2
Lap	2 x 3
Twin	3 x 5
Queen	4 x 5
King	5 x 5

2. Flip block on right to block on left. Match and pin seams. Sew with ¼" seam.

3. Pin and sew all blocks in rows.

4. Lay out rows. Press seams in opposite directions so seams lock.

5. Pin and sew rows together.

6. Press.

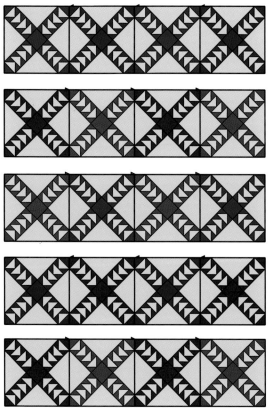

Sewing Star Borders

1. Trim selvages off 4½" First Border strips, and piece short ends together. Repeat with Second Border strips.

2. Sew First and Second Border strips together lengthwise with ¼" seam. Press seam toward darkest Border.

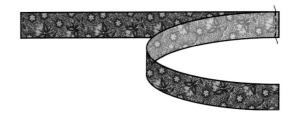

3. Measure sides of quilt top, and find an average. Cut two strips that measurement.

4. Measure top and bottom, and find an average. Cut two strips that measurement.

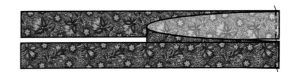

5. Pin and sew Borders to sides. Set seams, open, and press seams toward Borders.

6. Sew Stars to ends of top and bottom Borders. Press seams away from Stars.

7. Pin and sew Borders to top and bottom. Set seams, open, and press seams toward Borders.

8. Pin and sew optional Striped Borders to sides. *Striped Borders on antique quilts were usually not mitered.* Set seams, open, and press seams toward Striped Borders.

9. Pin and sew Striped Borders to top and bottom. Set seams, open, and press seams toward Striped Borders.

Light Geese
with Multiple Fabrics

Patricia Knoechel   *Twin*

Select these fabrics.

Two complimentary colors for two different sets of blocks, as blue and purple.

One Light Fabric for Geese

Choose one that coordinates with both, as a tone on tone.

One Side Triangle fabric

This fabric pulls the two blocks together. The sample is a contemporary, mottled piece of light medium fabric that has tones of both blue and purple.

Sky in eight Tone on Tone Values

Choose four for each block. The darkest values are also the Center squares. Each Sky gets progressively lighter toward the Corners.

Two Corner Triangle fabrics

One may be a medium value small scale print that ties the two colors together; the other may be a dark medium value. These two pieces touch each other in the finished quilt.

Use in Both

Geese	*Side Triangles*

Color One

Dark Sky	*Dark Medium*	*Medium*	*Light Medium*	*Corner Triangles*

Color Two

Dark Sky	*Dark Medium*	*Medium*	*Light Medium*	*Corner Triangles*

Color One   *17" x 17"*

Color Two   *17" x 17"*

Paste-Up Sheet – Multiple Fabrics

Make photo copies for Color One and Color Two

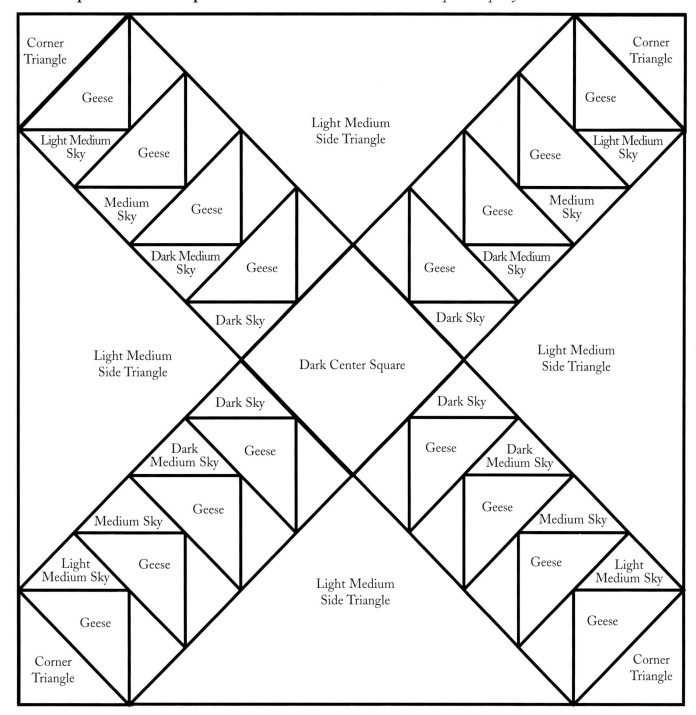

These measurements are for your Paste-Up Sheet only.

Cut swatches from your fabric and paste in place with a glue stick.

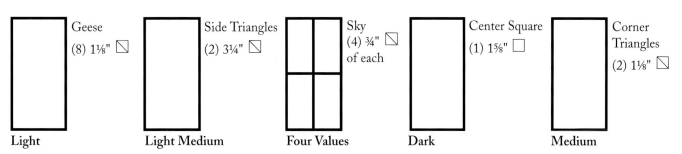

Geese
(8) 1⅛" ◺

Side Triangles
(2) 3¼" ◺

Sky
(4) ¾" ◺
of each

Center Square
(1) 1⅝" ☐

Corner
Triangles
(2) 1⅛" ◺

Light   **Light Medium**   **Four Values**   **Dark**   **Medium**

Color One

Color Two

Multiple Fabric Quilt

Cut strips selvage to selvage.
Cut sqs from strips. Left over strips can be cut into
smaller size squares on yardage chart.

	One Block	Four Block	Lap
Geese	¼ yd (4) 5½" sqs	⅝ yd (3) 5½" strips cut into (16) 5½" sqs	¾ yd (4) 5½" strips cut into (24) 5½" sqs
Side Triangles	½ yd (1) 13" sq	1 yd (2) 13" strips cut into (4) 13" sqs	1 yd (2) 13" strips cut into (6) 13" sqs
Color One	(4) different ¼ yd pieces Cut from each piece	(4) different ¼ yd pieces Cut from each piece	(4) different ¼ yd pieces Cut from each piece
Sky	(1) 7" sq	(2) 7" sqs	(3) 7" sqs
Center Square	(1) 4½" sq from darkest	(2) 4½" sqs from darkest	(3) 4½" sqs from darkest
Corner Triangles	⅛ yd (2) 4" sqs	⅛ yd (4) 4" sqs	⅛ yd (6) 4" sqs
Two Borders	¼ yd (2) 1½" strips	⅓ yd (4) 2" strips	⅓ yd (5) 2" strips
	⅓ yd (3) 3" strips	½ yd (4) 3½" strips	⅝ yd (5) 3 ½" strips
Color Two		(4) different ¼ yd pieces Cut from each piece	(4) different ¼ yd pieces Cut from each piece
Sky		(2) 7" sqs	(3) 7" sqs
Center Square		(2) 4½" sqs from darkest	(3) 4½" sqs from darkest
Corner Triangles		⅛ yd (4) 4" sqs	⅛ yd (6) 4" sqs
Binding	⅓ yd (3) 3" strips	½ yd (5) 3" strips	⅝ yd (6) 3" strips
Backing	1 yd	2 ½ yds	3 yds
Batting	36" x 36"	48" x 48"	48" x 66"

1 Block	1 Block 1 One Color	24" x 24"
4 Block	4 Blocks 2 Color One and 2 Color Two	42" x 42"
Lap	6 Blocks 3 Color One and 3 Color Two	42" x 60"
Twin	15 Blocks 7 Color One and 8 Color Two	66" x 100"
Queen	20 Blocks 10 Color One and 10 Color Two	90" x 107"
King	25 Blocks 12 Color One and 13 Color Two	108" x 108"

Twin	Queen	King
1 ½ yds (9) 5½" sqs cut into 　(60) 5½" sqs	2 yds (12) 5½" strips cut into 　(80) 5½" sqs	2 ½ yds (15) 5½" strips cut into 　(100) 5½" sqs
2 yds (5) 13" strips cut into 　(15) 13" sqs	2 ¾ yds (7) 13" strips cut into 　(20) 13" sqs	3 ½ yds (9) 13" strips cut into 　(25) 13" sqs
(4) different ⅝ yd pieces Cut from each piece (2) 7" strips cut into 　(7) 7" sqs (7) 4½" sqs from darkest	(4) different ⅝ yd pieces Cut from each piece (2) 7" strips cut into 　(10) 7" sqs (10) 4½" sqs from darkest	(4) different ¾ yd pieces Cut from each piece (2) 7" strips cut into 　(12) 7" sqs (12) 4½" sqs from darkest
⅓ yd (2) 4" strips cut into 　(14) 4" sqs	⅓ yd (2) 4" strips cut into 　(20) 4" sqs	½ yd (3) 4" strips cut into 　(24) 4" sqs
¾ yd (7) 3½" strips	1 ½ yds (8) 5½" strips	1 ¾ yds (9) 5½" strips
1 ½ yds (8) 5½" strips	2 ¼ yds (10) 7½" strips	2 ½ yds (11) 7½" strips
(4) different ⅝ yd pieces Cut from each piece (2) 7" strips cut into 　(8) 7" sqs (8) 4½" sqs from darkest	(4) different ⅝ yd pieces Cut from each piece (2) 7" strips cut into 　(10) 7" sqs (10) 4½" sqs from darkest	(4) different ¾ yd pieces Cut from each piece (3) 7" strips cut into 　(13) 7" sqs (13) 4½" sqs from darkest
⅓ yd (2) 4" strips cut into 　(16) 4" sqs	⅓ yd (2) 4" strips cut into 　(20) 4" sqs	½ yd (3) 4" strips cut into 　(26) 4" sqs
¾ yd (8) 3" strips	1 yd (10) 3" strips	1 yd (11) 3" strips
6 yds	8 ¼ yds	9 ½ yds
72" x 106"	98" x 114"	114" x 114"

Multiple Fabric Quilt

1. Place 5½" Geese squares right sides together to 7" Sky squares.

2. Sew 2" x 4" Light Geese, following detailed directions beginning on page 16.

Four Sky Values **Four Sky Values**

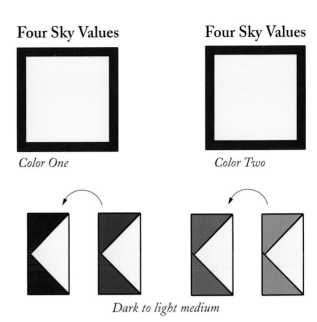

Color One *Color Two*

3. Stack Color One Geese in order by dark to light medium value, and divide into pairs.

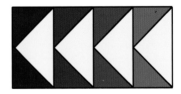

Dark to light medium

4. Assembly-line sew all pairs with accurate ¼" seam, crossing point as you stitch.

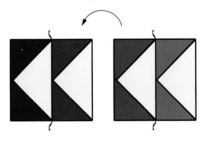

5. Sew pairs together into sets of four. Clip connecting threads.

6. Press seams from base toward point of Geese.

Sewing Color Two ¼eese Together

1. Stack Color Two Geese in order by dark to light medium value, and divide into pairs.

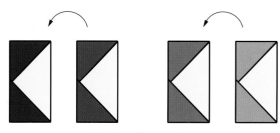

Dark to light medium

2. Assembly-line sew pairs together.

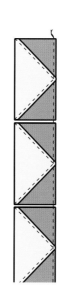

3. Open pairs, and sew together into sets of four.

4. Place on pressing mat wrong side up. Press seams toward base of Geese.

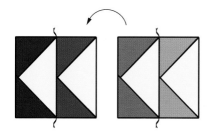

5. Press on right side, making certain there are no tucks at seams.

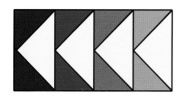

Sets of Four	Color One	Color Two
One Block Wallhanging	4	
Four Block Wallhanging	8	8
Lap	12	12
Twin	28	32
Queen	40	40
King	48	52

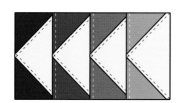

Finishing Block

1. Work on one color at a time. Follow detailed directions beginning on page 23.

2. Sew 4" Corner Triangles to Geese.

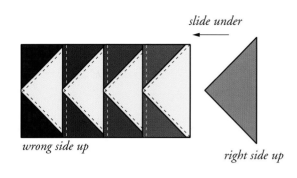

3. Sew 4½" Center Squares to Geese.

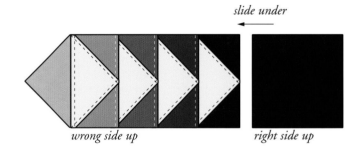

4. Sew blocks together with 13" Side Triangles.

5. Square up blocks.

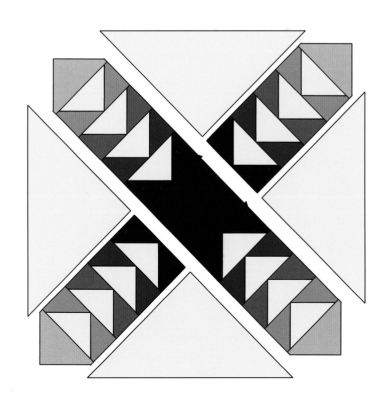

Sewing Top Together

1. Lay out blocks, alternating Color One and Color Two.

Block Layout	
Four Block Wallhanging	2 x 2
Lap	2 x 3
Twin	3 x 5
Queen	4 x 5
King	5 x 5

2. Flip block on right to block on left.

3. Match and pin seams. Sew with
   ¼" seam.

4. Sew blocks together into rows.

5. Pin and sew rows together, pressing
   seams in opposite directions.

6. Press.

Turn to page 72 for finishing.

Turn to page 72 for finishing.

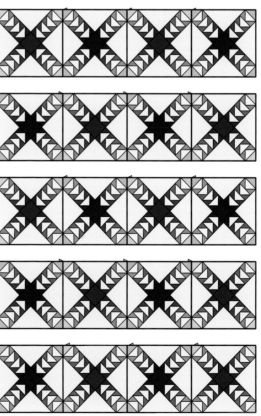

Dark Geese
with Three Fabrics

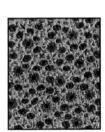

Select these fabrics.

One Medium Fabric

Begin with this fabric, which is used for the Side Triangles, and half of the Corner Triangles. Select a medium or large scale print with multiple colors. Pull remaining colors from this fabric that contrast and show off the design.

One Light Fabric

This fabric is used for Sky and Center Square, and should be a small scale print, or one that reads solid from a distance. As an alternate, the Center Square can be a fussy cut 4½" square cut on point in either light or dark. See page 11 for cutting instructions.

One Dark Fabric

This fabric is used for Geese and half of the Corner Triangles. It should contrast with the light, and also be a small scale or solid from a distance. Vary the texture between the light and dark.

Secondary Pattern and Borders

When blocks are joined together, Corner Triangles from dark and medium create a secondary pattern, which is repeated in the Borders. A straight fussy cut can also be used in the Borders. The One Block and Four Block Wallhangings have only two Borders in light and dark with Corner Patches. Larger quilts have an additional Third Border in medium.

Sue Bouchard   *Lap*

Geese   *Sky*   *Side Triangles*

Fussy Cut Detail

Finished Block   *17" x 17"*

46

Paste-Up Sheet – Three Fabrics

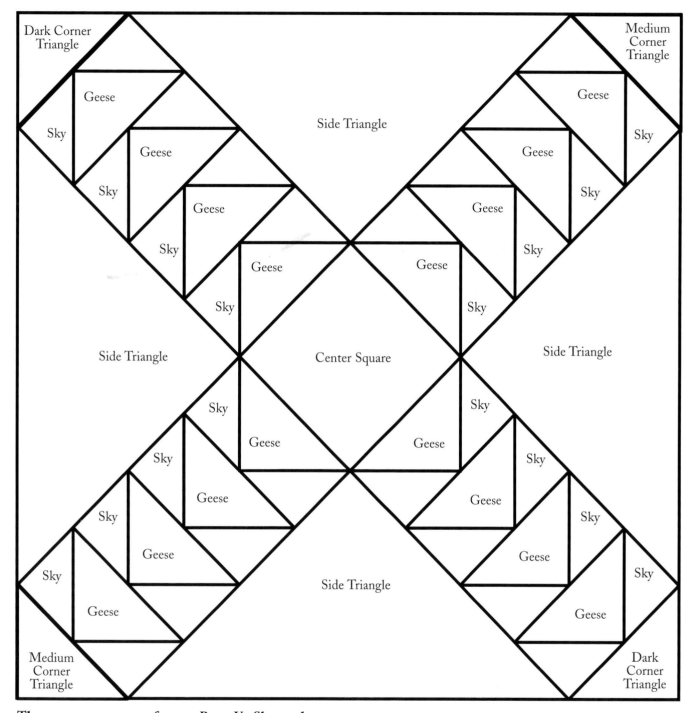

These measurements are for your Paste-Up Sheet only.

Cut swatches from your fabric and paste in place with a glue stick.

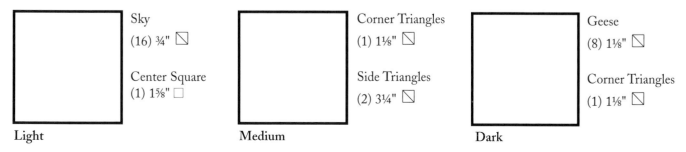

Light
Sky
(16) ¾" ◻

Center Square
(1) 1⅝" ☐

Medium
Corner Triangles
(1) 1⅛" ◻

Side Triangles
(2) 3¼" ◻

Dark
Geese
(8) 1⅛" ◻

Corner Triangles
(1) 1⅛" ◻

Three Fabric Quilt

Cut strips selvage to selvage.
Cut squares from strips. Left over strips can be cut into smaller size squares on yardage chart.

		One Block	Four Block	Lap
Dark Geese		**½ yd**	**1 yd**	**1 ¼ yds**
	Geese	(4) 5½" sqs	(3) 5½" strips cut into (16) 5½" sqs	(4) 5½" strips cut into (24) 5½" sqs
	Border	(2) 5½" sqs (2) 2½" strips	(2) 5½" sqs (4) 2½" strips	(2) 5½" sqs (5) 2½" strips
	Corner Triangles	(2) 4" sqs	(1) 4" strip cut into (4) 4" sqs	(1) 4" strip cut into (6) 4" sqs
Light Sky		**½ yd**	**1 ¼ yds**	**1 ¾ yds**
	Sky	(4) 7" sqs	(3) 7" strips cut into (16) 7" sqs	(5) 7" strips cut into (24) 7" sqs
	Center Square Or Fussy Cut	(1) 4½" sq	(1) 4½" strip cut into (4) 4½" sqs	(1) 4½" strip cut into (6) 4½" sqs
	Border	(2) 2½" strips	(4) 2½" strips	(5) 2½" strips
Medium Side Triangles		**½ yd**	**1 yd**	**1 ¾ yds**
	Side Triangles	(1) 13" sq	(2) 13" strips cut into (4) 13" sqs	(2) 13" strips cut into (6) 13" sqs
	Corner Triangles		(4) 4" sqs	(6) 4" sqs
	Border	(2) 5½" sqs	(2) 5½" sqs	(2) 5½" sqs (7) 4½" strips
Binding		**⅓ yd** (3) 3" strips	**½ yd** (5) 3" strips	**⅝ yd** (6) 3" strips
Backing		**1 yd**	**2 ½ yds**	**3 yds**
Batting		31" x 31"	48" x 48"	56" x 74"

1 Block	1 Block	25" x 25"
4 Block	4 Blocks	42" x 42"
Lap	6 Blocks	48" x 65"
Twin	15 Blocks	73" x 106"
Queen	20 Blocks	89" x 106"
King	25 Blocks	106" x 106"

Twin	Queen	King
3 yds	**3 ¾ yds**	**4 ½ yds**
(9) 5½" strips cut into	(12) 5½" strips cut into	(15) 5½" strips cut into
(60) 5½" sqs	(80) 5½" sqs	(100) 5½" sqs
(2) 4" strips cut into	(2) 4" strips cut into	(3) 4" strips cut into
(15) 4" sqs	(20) 4" sqs	(25) 4" sqs
(2) 9½" sqs	(2) 9½" sqs	(2) 9½" sqs
(7) 4½" strips	(9) 4½" strips	(10) 4½" strips
3 ½ yds	**4 ½ yds**	**5 ¼ yds**
(10) 7" strips cut into	(14) 7" strips cut into	(17) 7" strips cut into
(60) 7" sqs	(80) 7" sqs	(100) 7" sqs
(2) 4½" strips cut into	(2) 4½" strips cut into	(2) 4½" strips cut into
(15) 4½" sqs	(20) 4½" sqs	(25) 4½" sqs
(7) 4½" strips	(9) 4½" strips	(10) 4½" strips
3 ¾ yds	**4 ½ yds**	**5 ½ yds**
(5) 13" strips cut into	(7) 13" strips cut into	(9) 13" strips cut into
(15) 13" sqs	(20) 13" sqs	(25) 13" sqs
(2) 4" strips cut into	(2) 4" strips cut into	(3) 4" strips cut into
(15) 4" sqs	(20) 4" sqs	(25) 4" sqs
(2) 9½" sqs	(2) 9½" sqs	(2) 9½" sqs
(9) 4½" strips	(10) 4½" strips	(11) 4½" strips
⅞ yd	**1 yd**	**1 yd**
(9) 3" strips	(10) 3" strips	(11) 3" strips
7 yds	**8 ½ yds**	**10 yds**
81" x 115"	98" x 115"	115" x 115"

Making 2" x 4" Dark Geese

1. Place 5½" dark Geese square right sides together and centered on 7" light Sky square. Press.

Each set makes four Geese.

2. Place 6" x 12" ruler on squares so ruler touches all four corners. Draw diagonal line across squares.

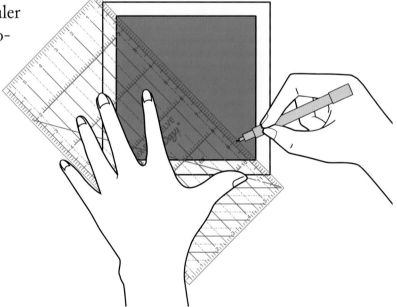

3. Pin.

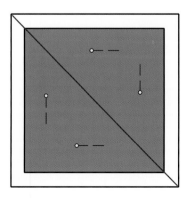

4. Sew **exactly** ¼" from drawn line. Use 15 stitches per inch or 2.0 on computerized machines. Assembly-line sew several squares.

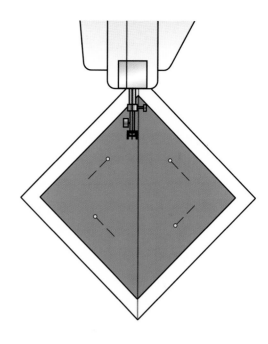

5. Turn and sew ¼" seam from second side of drawn line. Press to set seam.

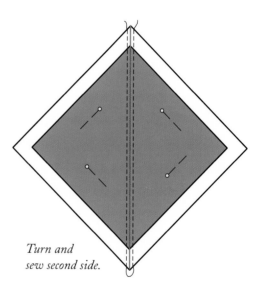

Turn and sew second side.

6. Remove pins. Cut on drawn line.

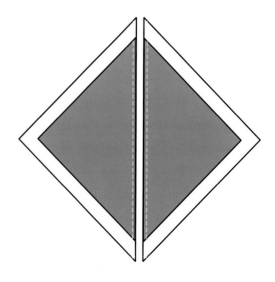

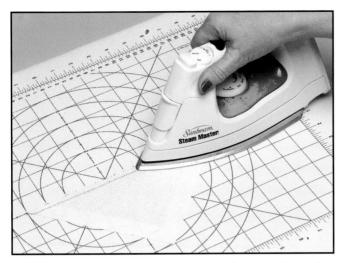

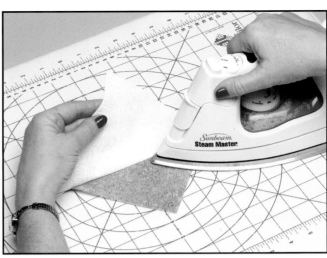

7. Place on pressing mat with **large triangle** on top. Press to set seam.

8. Open and press flat. Check that there are no tucks, and **seam is pressed toward larger triangle.**

9. Place pieces right sides together so that opposite fabrics touch with Geese matched to Sky. **Seams are parallel with each other.**

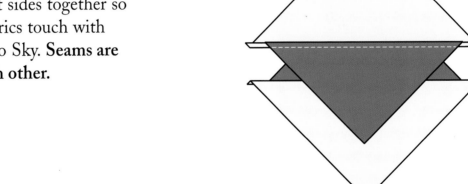

Seams are pressed toward larger triangle.

10. Match up outside edges. Notice that there is a gap between seams. **The seams do not lock.**

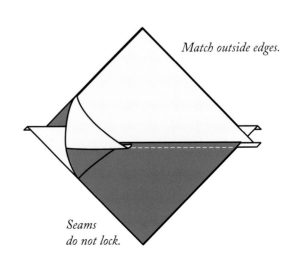

Match outside edges.

Seams do not lock.

11. Draw a diagonal line across seams. Pin.

12. Sew ¼" from both sides of drawn line. Hold seam flat with stiletto so seams do not flip. Press to set seam.

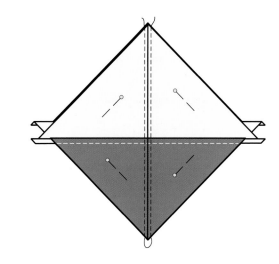

13. Cut on the drawn line.

14. Clip the seam allowance to the vertical seam midway between the horizontal seams. This allows the seam allowance to be pressed away from Geese.

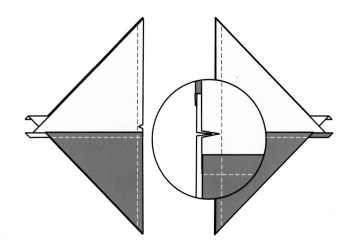

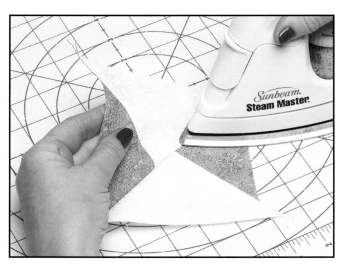

15. From right side, press into one Geese. Turn and press into second Geese.

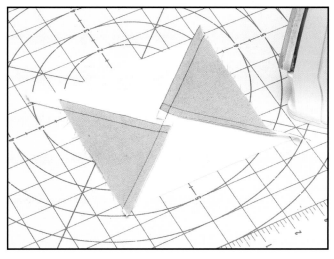

16. Turn over and press on wrong side. At clipped seam, fabric is pressed away from Geese.

Squaring Up With Geese Ruler

1. Place Geese on small cutting mat so you can rotate mat as you cut.

2. Use the Large Flying Geese ruler. Line up ruler's 2" x 4" **red lines** on 45° sewn lines. Line up dotted line with peak of triangle for the ¼" seam allowance.

3. Cut block in half to separate the two patches.

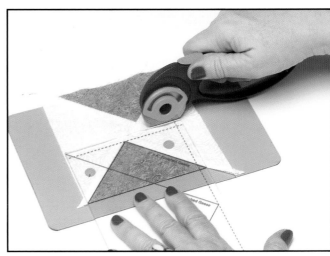

Cut block in half.

4. Trim off excess fabric. Hold ruler securely on fabric so it will not shift while cutting.

5. Turn patch around. **Do not turn ruler.** Trim off excess fabric.

If you do not have a Geese ruler, turn to page 21 for alternate instructions.

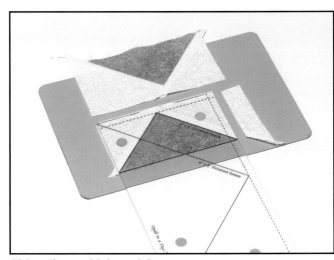

Trim off excess fabric on right.

Total Number of Geese Needed	
1 Block Wallhanging	16
4 Block Wallhanging	64
Lap	96
Twin	240
Queen	320
King	400

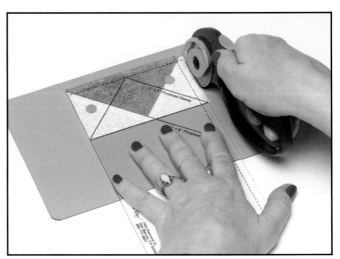

Turn patch. Trim off excess on right.

Sewing Dark Geese Together

1. Divide Geese into two equal stacks.

2. Flip Goose patch on right to Goose patch on left. Match outside edges.

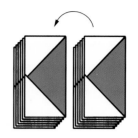

3. Hold seam flat with stiletto. Sew accurate ¼" seam, crossing point as you stitch.

4. Check to see that point is "crisp" on right side.

5. Assembly-line sew all Geese into pairs. Clip connecting threads.

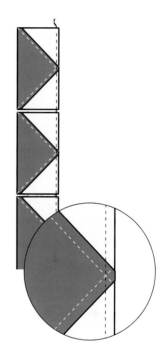

6. Divide into two equal stacks.

7. Sew together into sets of four. Clip connecting threads.

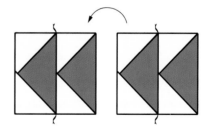

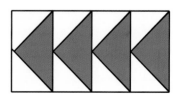

Sets of Four	
1 Block Wallhanging	4
4 Block Wallhanging	16
Lap	24
Twin	60
Queen	80
King	100

Pressing Geese

1. Place on pressing mat wrong side up. Press seams from base toward point of Geese.

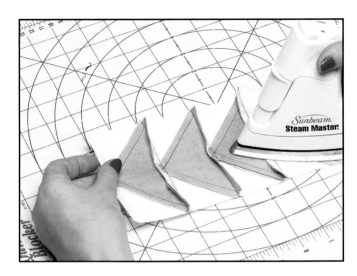

2. Press on right side, making certain there are no tucks at seams.

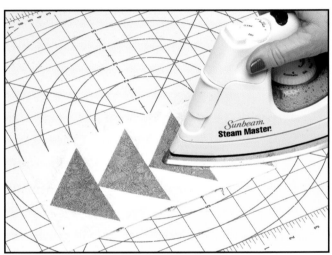

Three Color Dark Geese Pointing Away from Center Square

1. Cut dark and medium 4" squares for Corner Triangles in half on one diagonal, and stack right side up. Keep different color triangles in two separate stacks.

   One Block Wallhanging: Sew all dark Corner Triangles to Geese.

Dark   *Medium*

2. Divide Geese into two equal stacks.

3. Turn Geese **wrong side up**. Place Corner Triangles next to Geese **right sides up**.

4. Slide Corners under Geese, and center.

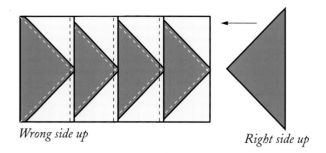

Wrong side up   *Right side up*

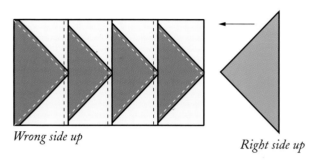

Wrong side up   *Right side up*

5. Assembly-line sew with ¼" seam, keeping tips equal on outside edges.

6. Clip connecting threads.

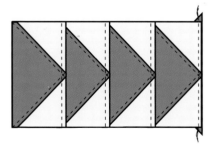

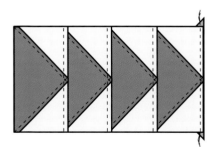

Pressing Geese Seams

1. Place on pressing mat with triangles on top.

2. Set seams, open, and press.
   Seams are pressed toward Triangle.

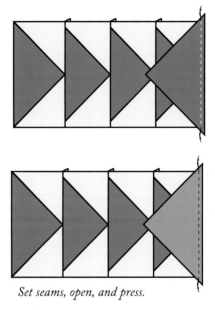

Set seams, open, and press.

3. Line up Geese ruler with outside edges of Geese, and trim off tips.

   Alternate: Use 6" Square Up ruler.

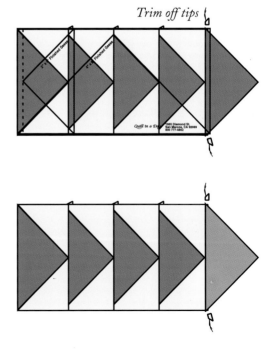

Trim off tips

Sewing Center Squares with Geese

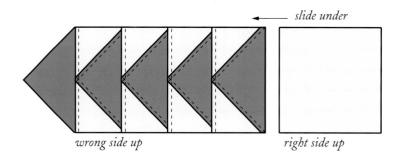

1. Stack 4½" Center Squares or fussy cuts right side up. Stack an equal number of Geese with **dark Corner Triangles** wrong side up.

2. Slide Center Squares under Geese.

wrong side up   *right side up*

slide under

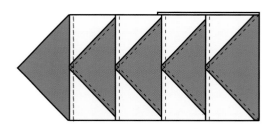

3. Match outside edges, and assembly-line sew.

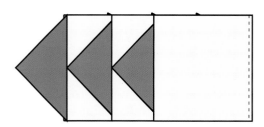

4. Set seams with Center Square on top. Open, and press seam flat. Clip connecting threads.

5. Sew Geese with dark Corner Triangles on opposite side of Center Square.

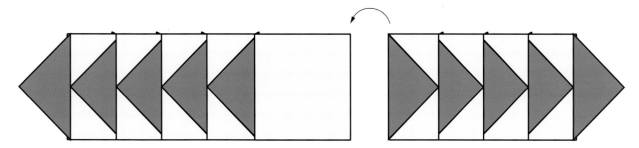

6. Set seams with Center Square on top. Open, and press seams flat. Seams will be toward Center Square.

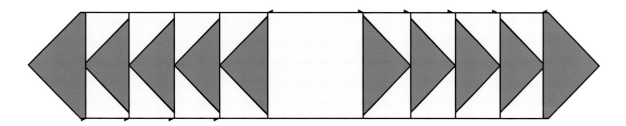

Sewing Block Together

1. Find the stretchy edges of each 13" Side Triangle square. Stack right sides up with stretch at top and bottom. With 6" x 24" ruler, cut on both diagonals into quarters.

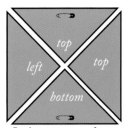

2. Separate Triangles into four equal stacks. **Mark all top and bottom triangles with safety pins. Keep safety pins in block until after top is sewn together.**

Its important to keep triangles in order because they stretch in opposite directions.

3. Place Geese with Medium Corner Triangles in center of stacks. Work on one half at a time.

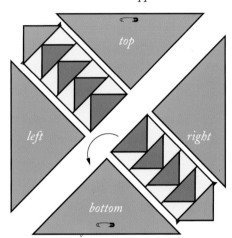

4. Flip Geese to Side Triangle on left. Match top edges and sides. Side Triangle fabric will stick out on bottom edge.

5. Assembly-line sew, using stiletto to hold seams flat.

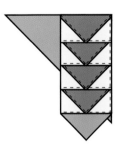

Edges of Side Triangles are on the bias, and should always be sewn on the bottom to avoid stretching.

6. Flip remaining Side Triangle to Geese. Match top edges and sides. Pin in place.

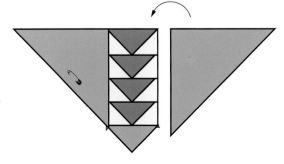

7. **Turn over to wrong side.** Sew from Triangle Corner, using stiletto to hold seams flat.

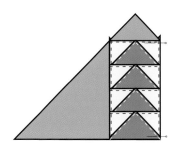

8. Place on pressing mat with Side Triangles on top. Press to set seams.

9. Open, and press flat. Seams will be toward Side Triangles.

10. Lay out three units. Place Side Triangles in order with center strip.

11. Flip Center to left. Match and pin center seams. Pin Geese to Side Triangles. Assembly-line sew with Side Triangles on bottom, holding seams flat with stiletto.

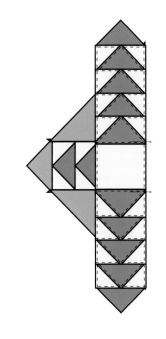
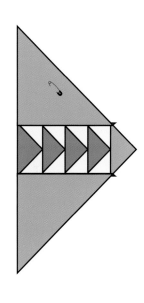

12. Flip Center Strip to remaining Side Triangles. Pin, and assembly-line sew with side Triangles on bottom.

13. Place on pressing mat right side up. Press to set seams. Open, and press seams flat. Center seams will be toward Side Triangles.

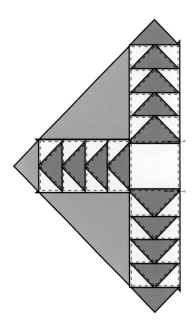

Squaring Up Blocks

1. Using grid lines, place block straight on cutting mat. Place 6" x 24" ruler on side of block. Line up ruler's ¼" lines on seams. Line up diagonal line down center of Geese. Straighten side.

2. Turn and trim remaining sides. Note measurement of block with lines on grid.

3. Trim all blocks consistently.

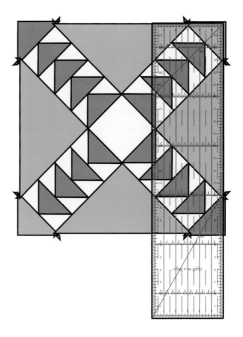

Sewing Top Together

1. Lay out blocks. Place Side Triangles with safety pins at top and bottom. **Check secondary pattern created by dark and medium Corner Triangles.**

2. Flip block on right to block on left.

3. Match and pin seams. Sew with ¼" seam.

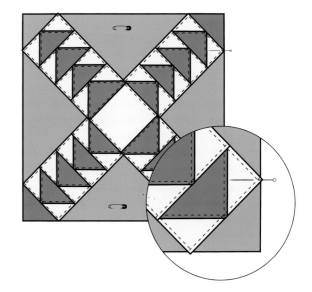

Block Layout	
4 Block Wallhanging	2 x 2
Lap	2 x 3
Twin	3 x 5
Queen	4 x 5
King	5 x 5

4. Pin and sew all blocks in row together. Press seams in one direction.

5. Lay out rows with seams going in opposite directions.

6. Pin and sew rows together.

7. Press.

Turn to page 72 for finishing.

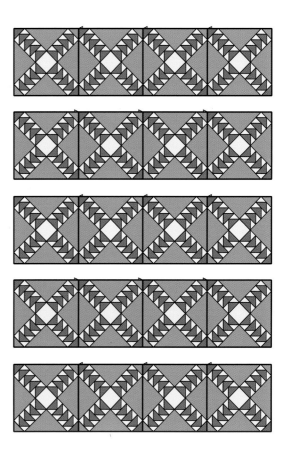

Sewing Borders

Measurements for larger quilts are in parenthesis.

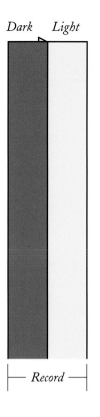

Dark   *Light*

1. **Wallhanging:** Short ends of 2½" strips do not need to be pieced together.

2. **Lap:** Cut one strip of 2½" light and 2½" dark in half. Piece short ends of 2½" half strips to short ends of whole strips.

3. **Larger Quilts:** Trim selvages on 4½" light and dark strips and sew short ends together.

4. Sew 2½" (4½") Border strips together. Make four sets longer than the sides of the quilt. Press seams toward darkest fabric.

5. Measure width of sewn together strips.

Record

Use this measurement for patchwork or size for fussy cut.

Making Border Corners

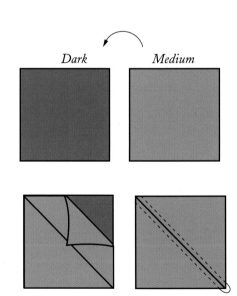

Dark   *Medium*

1. Place two sets of 5½" (9½") squares dark and medium right sides together.

2. Draw a diagonal line. Sew ¼" from both sides of diagonal line.

3. Cut into fourths on both diagonal lines.

4. Press seams to darkest fabric.

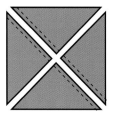

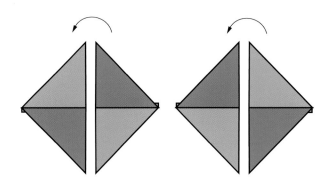

5. Sort into two sets of blocks.

6. Flip piece on right to piece on left. Match center seams, and assembly-line sew.

7. Press seams to one side.

8. Square up Corners to same measurement as width of Border strips. Diagonal lines should go into corners of blocks.

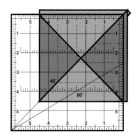

9. Cut four Borders same size as quilt top.

10. Sew Borders to two opposite sides of quilt top.

11. Sew Corners to top and bottom Border strips. Sew to quilt top.

Turn to page 72 for finishing.

Light and Dark Geese in Positive/Negative Fabrics

Two blocks are made for the Positive Negative Quilt, with a total reversal of color from each other. When blocks are sewn together, a strong geometric design is created. For a most effective quilt, select two small scale prints that read solid from a distance.

One Light Fabric

The Positive Block is mainly light fabric, including Geese, Side Triangles, and Corner Triangles. Sky and Center Square are made from the dark fabric. **Light Geese fly away from a dark Center Square.** A narrow light First Border frames and settles the design.

One Dark Fabric

The Negative Block is mainly dark fabric including Geese, Side Triangles, and Corner Triangles. Sky and Center Square are made from the light fabric. **Dark Geese fly away from a light Center Square.** A dark Second Border and Binding complete the graphic quilt.

Positive Block

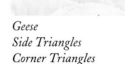

Geese
Side Triangles
Corner Triangles

Sky
Center Square

Negative Block

Geese
Side Triangles
Corner Triangles

Sky
Center Square

Positive Block

Negative Block

Paste-Up Sheet – Two Fabrics, Positive Negative   *Make photocopies for Positive and Negative Blocks.*

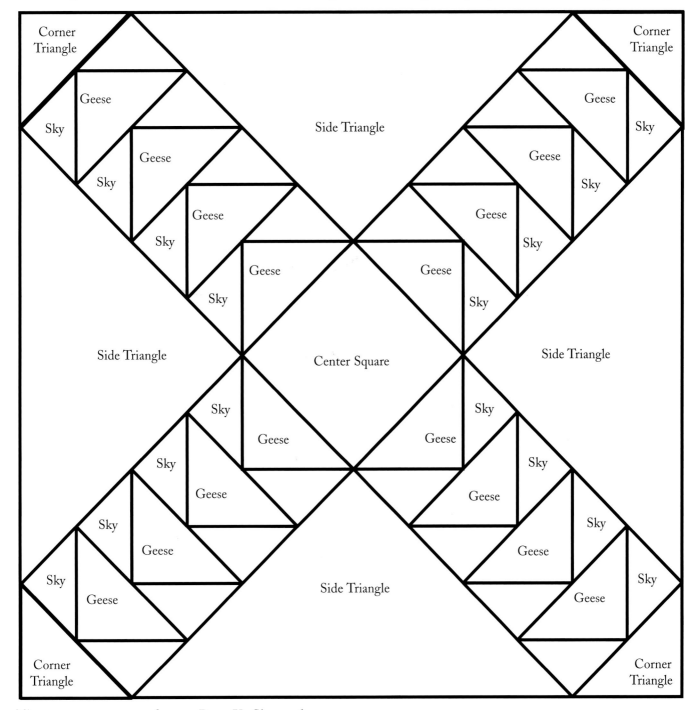

These measurements are for your Paste-Up Sheet only.

Cut swatches from your fabric and paste in place with a glue stick.

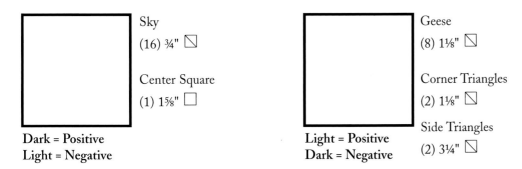

Sky
(16) ¾" ◻

Center Square
(1) 1⅝" ▢

Dark = Positive
Light = Negative

Geese
(8) 1⅛" ◻

Corner Triangles
(2) 1⅛" ◻

Side Triangles
(2) 3¼" ◻

Light = Positive
Dark = Negative

Positive Block

Negative Block

Positive Negative Quilt

Cut strips selvage to selvage.
Cut squares from strips. Left over strips can be
cut into smaller size squares on yardage chart.

		Four Block	Lap
Light		**1 ¾ yds**	**2 yds**
	Side Triangles	(1) 13" strip cut into (2) 13" sqs	(1) 13" strip cut into (3) 13" sqs
	Geese	(2) 5½" strips cut into (8) 5½" sqs	(2) 5½" strips cut into (12) 5½" sqs
	Sky	(2) 7" strips cut into (8) 7" sqs	(2) 7" strips cut into (12) 7" sqs
	Center Square	(2) 4½" sqs	(3) 4½" sqs
	Corner Triangles	(4) 4" sqs	(6) 4" sqs
	First Border	(4) 2" strips	(5) 3½" strips
Dark		**2 yds**	**2 ¾ yds**
	Side Triangles	(1) 13" strip cut into (2) 13" sqs	(1) 13" strip cut into (3) 13" sqs
	Geese	(2) 5½" strips cut into (8) 5½" sqs	(2) 5½" strips cut into (12) 5½" sqs
	Sky	(2) 7" strips cut into (8) 7" sqs	(2) 7" strips cut into (12) 7" sqs
	Center Square	(2) 4½" sqs	(3) 4½" sqs
	Corner Triangles	(4) 4" sqs	(6) 4" sqs
	Second Border	(4) 3" strips	(6) 5½" strips
	Binding	(5) 3" strips	(6) 3" strips
Backing		**2 ½ yds**	**3 yds**
Batting		48" x 48"	56" x 72"

4 Block	4 Blocks 2 Positive and 2 Negative	42" x 42"	
Lap	6 Blocks 3 Positive and 3 Negative	50" x 66"	
Twin	15 Blocks 7 Positive and 8 Negative	66" x 100"	
Queen	20 Blocks 10 Positive and 10 Negative	90" x 107"	
King	25 Blocks 12 Positive and 13 Negative	108" x 108"	

Twin	Queen	King
4 ¼ yds	**5 ¾ yds**	**6 yds**
(3) 13" strips cut into (7) 13" sqs	(4) 13" strips cut into (10) 13" sqs	(4) 13" strips cut into (12) 13" sqs
(4) 5½" strips cut into (28) 5½" sqs	(6) 5½" strips cut into (40) 5½" sqs	(7) 5½" strips cut into (48) 5½" sqs
(6) 7" strips cut into (32) 7" sqs	(7) 7" strips cut into (40) 7" sqs	(8) 7" strips cut into (48) 7" sqs
(1) 4½" strip cut into (8) 4½" sqs	(2) 4½" strips cut into (10) 4½" sqs	(2) 4½" strips cut into (12) 4½" sqs
(2) 4" strips cut into (14) 4" sqs	(2) 4" strips cut into (20) 4" sqs	(3) 4" strips cut into (24) 4" sqs
(7) 3½" strips	(8) 5½" strips	(9) 5½" strips
5 ¼ yds	**7 ½ yds**	**8 ¼ yds**
(3) 13" strips cut into (8) 13" sqs	(4) 13" strips cut into (10) 13" sqs	(5) 13" strips cut into (13) 13" sqs
(4) 5½" strips cut into (32) 5½" sqs	(6) 5½" strips cut into (40) 5½" sqs	(7) 5½" strips cut into (52) 5½" sqs
(5) 7" strips cut into (28) 7" sqs	(7) 7" strips cut into (40) 7" sqs	(8) 7" strips cut into (52) 7" sqs
(1) 4½" strip cut into (7) 4½" sqs	(2) 4½" strips cut into (10) 4½" sqs	(2) 4½" strips cut into (13) 4½" sqs
(2) 4" strips cut into (16) 4" sqs	(2) 4" strips cut into (20) 4" sqs	(3) 4" strips cut into (26) 4" sqs
(8) 5½" strips	(10) 7½" strips	(11) 7½" strips
(8) 3" strips	(10) 3" strips	(11) 3" strips
6 yds	**8 ¼ yds**	**9 ½ yds**
74" x 108"	98" x 115"	114" x 114"

Making Negative Blocks

Negative Block	
Dark	**Light**
13" squares for Side Triangles	7" squares for Sky
5½" squares for Geese	4½" squares for Center
4" squares for Corner Triangles	

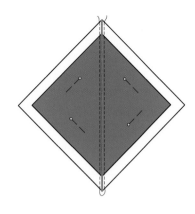

1. Sort squares into two separate piles.

2. Follow detailed directions beginning on page 50. The negative block is similar to making a Three Fabric block, substituting dark fabric for medium fabric.

3. Place 5½" dark Geese squares right sides together to 7" light Sky. Sew 2" x 4" dark Geese.

4. Cut 4" dark squares for Corner Triangles in half on diagonal and **sew to point of Geese**, page 57.

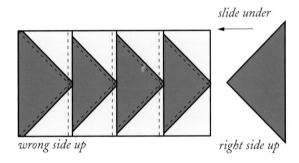

slide under

wrong side up   *right side up*

5. Sew 4½" light Center Squares to base of dark Geese, page 59. **Geese fly away from Center.**

6. Sew blocks together with 13" dark Side Triangles, page 60.

7. Square up blocks, page 62.

Making Positive Blocks

Positive Block	
Dark	**Light**
7" squares for Sky	13" squares for Side Triangles
4½" squares for Center	5½" squares for Geese
	4" squares for Corner Triangles

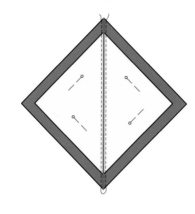

1. Sort squares into two separate piles.

2. Place 5½" light Geese squares right sides together to 7" dark Sky squares.

3. Sew sets of four light Geese following detailed directions from page 16 to 23.

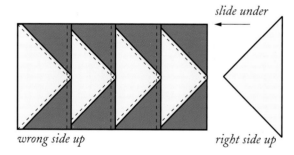

slide under

wrong side up   *right side up*

4. Cut 4" light squares for Corner Triangles in half on diagonal. **Sew Triangles to point of Geese.** Press seams toward Triangle, and trim tips.

5. Stack equal number of Geese with 4½" dark Center Squares. **Point Geese away from Center Square,** and sew together. Press seams toward Center Square.

6. Sew blocks together with 13" light Side Triangles.

7. Square up blocks.

8. Lay out blocks, alternating between the two.

9. Pin and sew together, following directions on page 45.

Finishing Your Quilt

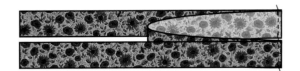

1. Cut Borders to desired sizes. Refer to Yardage Charts. Trim selvages.

2. Assembly-line sew all short ends together into long pieces for each fabric.

3. Cut First Border pieces the average length of both sides. Pin and sew to sides. Fold out and press seams toward Border.

4. Measure the width and cut Border pieces for the top and bottom. Pin and sew. Press seams toward the Border.

5. Repeat with any additional Borders.

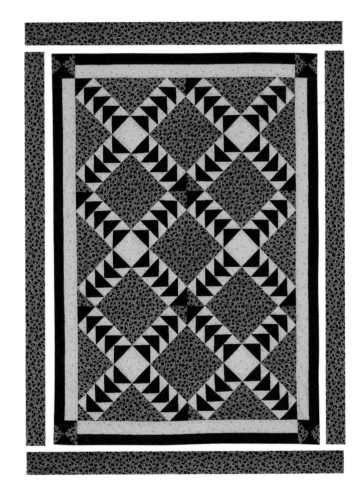

6. Spread out the Backing on a large table or floor area with the right side down. Clamp the fabric to the edge of the table with quilt clips or tape the Backing to the floor. Do not stretch the Backing.

7. Layer the batting on top of the Backing, and pat flat.

8. With the quilt top right side up, center on the Backing. Smooth until all layers are flat. Clamp or tape outside edges.

9. Choose between grid quilting, page 73 - 74, or free motion quilting, page 75.

Marking Grid on Quilt

1. Place 6" x 24" ruler on Side Triangle. Line up ruler between Geese.

2. Firmly push Hera marker along edge of ruler, and mark crease for quilting lines.

3. Mark crease lines in both directions.

Safety Pinning

1. Use 1" safety pins. Safety pin through all layers in the center of every Geese and Side Triangles every three to five inches. Pin away from marked lines.

2. Catch tip of pin in grooves on pinning tool, and close pins.

3. Use pinning tool to open pins when removing them. Store pins opened.

Dashed lines represent all quilting lines.

"Stitch in the Ditch" in Side Triangles and Borders

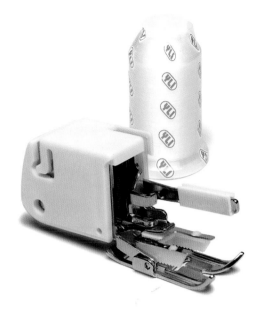

1. Thread your machine with matching thread or invisible thread. If you use invisible thread, loosen your top tension. Match the bobbin thread to the Backing.

2. Attach your walking foot, and lengthen the stitch to 8 to 10 stitches per inch or 3.5 on computerized machines.

3. Place hands on quilt in triangular shape, and spread seams open.

4. Start quilting between Geese and Side Triangles at any point, and stitch continuously in diagonal lines, pivoting and turning with needle down.

5. Continue quilting until all the seams and Borders are stitched.

Quilting with Darning Foot

1. "Stitch in the Ditch" between Sky and Side Triangles and Borders.

2. Select a stencil approximately 6" square. Center on Side Triangles, and trace lines with marking pencil.

3. Attach darning foot to sewing machine. Drop feed dogs or cover feed dogs with a plate. No stitch length is required as you control the length. Use a fine needle and invisible or regular thread in the top and regular thread to match the Backing in the bobbin. Loosen top tension if using invisible thread.

4. Place hands flat on sides of marking. Bring bobbin thread up on line. Lock stitch and clip thread tails.

5. Free motion stitch around design, starting at the top. Lock stitch and cut threads.

Binding

Use a walking foot attachment and regular thread on top and in the bobbin to match the Binding.

1. Square off the selvage edges, and sew 3" strips together lengthwise.

2. Fold and press in half with wrong sides together.

3. Line up the raw edges of the folded Binding with the raw edges of the quilt in the middle of one side.

4. Begin stitching 4" from the end of the Binding. Sew with 10 stitches per inch, or 3.0 to 3.5 stitch length on computerized machines.

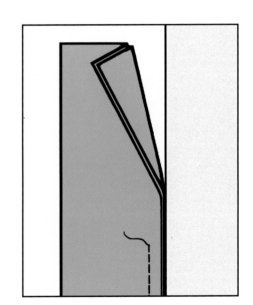

5. At the corner, stop the stitching ¼" from the edge with the needle in the fabric. Raise the presser foot and turn the quilt to the next side. Put the foot back down.

6. Stitch backwards ¼" to the edge of the Binding, raise the foot, and pull the quilt forward slightly.

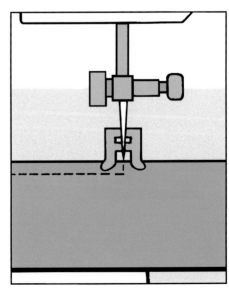

7. Fold the Binding strip straight up on the diagonal. Fingerpress the diagonal fold.

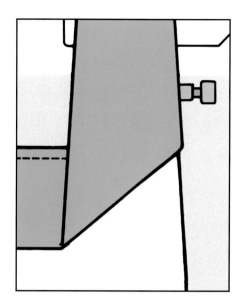

8. Fold the Binding strip straight down with the diagonal fold underneath. Line up the top of the fold with the raw edge of the Binding underneath.

9. Begin sewing from the edge.

10. Continue stitching and mitering the orners around the outside of the quilt.

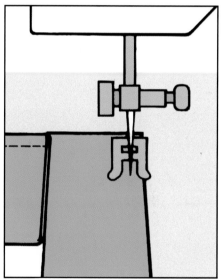

11. Stop stitching 4" from where the ends will overlap.

12. Line up the two ends of Binding. Trim the excess with a ½" overlap.

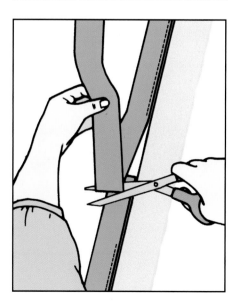

13. Open out the folded ends and pin right sides together. Sew a ¼" seam.

14. Continue to stitch the Binding in place.

15. Trim the batting and Backing up to the raw edges of the Binding.

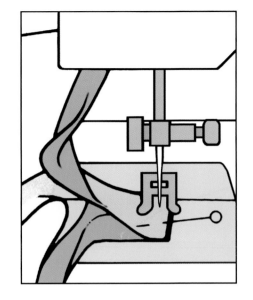

16. Fold the Binding to the back side of the quilt. Pin in place so that the folded edge on the Binding covers the stitching line. Tuck in the excess fabric at each miter on the diagonal.

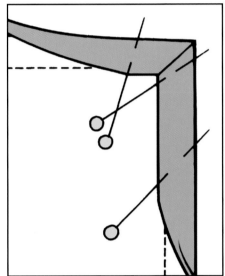

17. From the right side, "stitch in the ditch" using invisible thread on the front side, and a bobbin thread to match the Binding on the back side. Catch the folded edge of the Binding on the back side with the stitching.

Optional: Hand stitch Binding in place.

18. Sew an identification label on the Back.

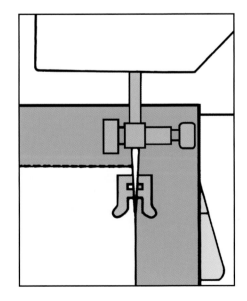

Index

Alice Borg   *42" x 58"*

Order Information

Quilt in a Day books offer a wide range of techniques and are directed toward a variety of skill levels. If you do not have a quilt shop in your area, you may write or call for a complete catalog and current price list of all books and patterns published by Quilt in a Day®, Inc.

Quilt in a Day®, Inc. • 1955 Diamond Street • San Marcos, CA 92069

1 800 777-4852 • Fax: (760) 591-4424 • www.quiltinaday.com

Carol Selepec skillfully quilted graceful feathers in the Side Triangles and Border, and "stitched in the ditch" around the Geese.